I KNOW AMERICA

# Our
# Postal
# System

### Eileen Lucas

THE MILLBROOK PRESS
Brookfield, Connecticut

Cover photograph courtesy of Gamma Liaison (© Roy Gumpel)

Photographs courtesy of Photo Researchers: pp. 4
(© Jeff Isaac Greenberg), 25, 27 (top © Jan Halaska,
bottom © Porterfield/Chickering), 29 (© James Holmes/
Science Photo Library), 30 (© Lawrence Migdale);
Stock Montage: p. 6; Corbis-Bettmann: pp. 10, 12, 13
(both), 14, 35; Bettmann: p. 16; Culver Pictures, Inc.:
p. 17; Brown Brothers: pp. 18, 19, 21; UPI/Corbis-
Bettmann: pp. 20, 39; U. S. Postal Service: p. 32;
Gamma Liaison: pp. 34 (© Roy Gumpel), 36 (Hulton
Getty Images), 40, 41 (© Porter Gifford 1993)

Library of Congress Cataloging-in-Publication Data
Lucas, Eileen.
Our postal system / Eileen Lucas.
p.   cm. — (I know America)
Includes bibliographical references and index.
Summary: Explores the history of the United States
Postal Service, discussing the processing of mail,
postal employees, stamps, and letter writing.
ISBN 0-7613-0966-7 (lib. bdg.)
1. Postal service—United States—Juvenile
literature. [1. Postal service.] I. Title.
II. Series.
HE6371.L83   1999
383'.4973—dc21   98-23316   CIP   AC

Published by The Millbrook Press, Inc.
2 Old New Milford Road
Brookfield, Connecticut  06804

5 4 3 2 1

# CONTENTS

# C H A P T E R

# PAPYRUS AND PENNY POSTS

Have you sent or received mail lately? It's almost certain that someone in your family has. You may have sent a thank-you note for a gift, or received a birthday party invitation in the mail. Maybe your mom or dad received a reminder that you have a doctor's or dentist's appointment coming up, or maybe they received a bill from a department store. Someone in your family may subscribe to magazines or newspapers that are delivered by mail.

Hardly a day goes by that the average American household does not use the Postal Service in some way. In fact, over 600 million pieces of mail are delivered to homes and businesses in the United States each working day. The Postal Service is so much a part of our lives that we might take it for granted. But there would definitely be something important missing if it were gone.

The postal system—the way in which we send and receive mail—has been around for a long time. The rulers of ancient civilizations had to figure out ways to get important messages from one place to another. In

5

some cases, fast runners carried messages they had memorized for their rulers. As written languages were developed, messages were written down on clay or bronze tablets, or on skins of animals or sheets of papyrus.

About 500 B.C., a Greek writer named Herodotus described the postal system of Persia. "There is no mortal thing faster than these messengers," he said. "Neither snow nor rain nor heat nor gloom of night stays these couriers from the swift completion of their appointed rounds." These words were later carved in stone on the front of the General Post Office in New York City.

The ancient Romans had a well-developed postal system as well. Communication across great distances was needed to hold their empire together. There was also a vast communication network in China that was described by the explorer Marco Polo in the 1200s. The Mayans and Aztecs in Central America had systems, too, for delivering messages and packages long ago.

At first most postal systems were just for rulers. In time, wealthy merchants also began to use the system. Later, ordinary people could use the system, *if* they could afford it.

In the 1600s, the London Penny Post was developed in England. Letters could be mailed anywhere in London for a penny. That penny might be paid either by the person who sent the mail or by the person who received it. Outside of London, the cost to mail a letter

## THE NATIONAL POSTAL MUSEUM

The National Postal Museum can be found in Washington, D.C. It is located in a building that was once the post office for that city. The museum holds many stamps and other objects relating to the mail. A stagecoach and several airmail planes show some of the ways that mail has been moved. Old letters and photographs and other interesting items can also be seen. Visitors can learn about the earliest history of the United States postal system. They can also find out about what's new and exciting in the Postal Service today. A trip to the Postal Museum is like a walk through America's history.

usually depended on the number of sheets of paper used, and the distance the letter was going.

When colonists came from England and other countries to the New World, they wanted to communicate with the family and business partners they had left behind. As time went on, they needed to communicate with people in other colonies as well. The story of how an American postal system developed is an important part of the story of how America itself developed.

# CHAPTER 2

# AMERICA BUILDS A POSTAL SYSTEM

When the earliest colonists came to the New World, getting mail back "home" was a difficult business indeed. Even writing a letter was difficult, because paper was expensive and hard to get. Once written, a letter was folded and sealed with a bit of wax. An address was written on the outside of the letter. This would include the recipient's name and town and maybe a place in that town to which the letter should be delivered, like a tavern or other business. Few streets had names, and houses were not numbered.

These letters were then given to ships' captains. On either side of the ocean, mail was deposited at taverns and coffee houses. It was up to people to come and look for their mail at such places. When they found a letter waiting for them, they usually had to pay to receive it. Sometimes this meant that a person could not claim a letter that was written to them because they couldn't afford it. As you can imagine, few people received mail very often.

Mail carriers in colonial times and in the early years of the United States had a difficult and often dangerous job. This mail carrier of the 1790s was fortunate to have a road on which to travel.

## The First Post Office

The first official post office in America was the tavern of a man named Richard Fairbanks in Boston. In 1639 it was named the official collection point for mail going to and from England. When ships docked in Boston Harbor, any mail they carried was brought to Fairbanks's tavern. When ships departed, they picked up any mail that had been left in a sack with Mr. Fairbanks.

By the early 1700s, there were a handful of postal riders who delivered mail between post offices in the various colonies on horseback. These early mail carriers faced many difficulties. The colonies were mostly made up of towns and smaller settlements along the Atlantic coast. There were few roads through the many miles of wilderness between these isolated settlements. Riders often used the same trails that Native Americans had walked on foot. In bad weather, these trails could be blocked by mud, fallen trees, or flooded rivers. If a rider got hurt, he might be many miles from any help. Sometimes postal riders were robbed by thieves looking for money that had been sent in the mail. When the mail made it through, colonists often grumbled about having to pay for the service. Many colonists looked on the official British postal rates as a form of taxation, and the colonists didn't like taxation. As much as possible, they avoided paying postage, mostly by sending mail by private rather than official carriers.

## A Printer for Postmaster

In 1753 a Philadelphia printer named Benjamin Franklin was one of two men given the job of joint postmaster general over much of the American colonies. Franklin was responsible for making many improvements in the postal system. By finding better routes, he shortened the amount of time it took for mail to get from one place to another. He allowed newspapers to be sent free from one printer to another, which increased the spread of news throughout the colonies. He also helped the postal system collect more money.

In 1774 the British government fired Franklin because he was helping the colonists who wanted to break away from England. When these colonists established the American post office the next year, they gave Franklin his job back. Because of all he did, Benjamin Franklin has become known as the "Father of the United States Postal Service."

After the Revolutionary War, the new American government expanded the postal system that Franklin and other colonists had developed. It cost six cents to

Benjamin Franklin was one of two men given the job of joint postmaster general over much of the American colonies. He made many improvements to the existing postal system.

send a one-page letter up to 30 miles. The cost went up to twenty-five cents if the letter was going 450 miles. This was very expensive, considering that few people earned very much money at all. Individuals still had to go looking for their mail at post offices, unless they lived in the few large cities of the new country. City dwellers could pay letter carriers up to two cents a letter (in addition to mailing cost) to have their mail delivered to their homes.

Beyond large cities, mail delivery was still a very difficult business. In 1799, it was noted that during the winter it took twenty-two days for the mail to travel the 646 miles from Lexington, Massachusetts, to Philadelphia, Pennsylvania.

## A Time of Many Changes

By the early 1800s, stagecoaches had joined horses and riders in carrying the mail between some post offices. Soon the newly developed steamboats were also being used. As railroad lines were laid between the more populated areas of the East, mail was carried on trains, too.

As America grew rapidly during the 1800s, many people thought that a good mail system was one thing that would help hold the country together. In 1829 the postmaster general became a member of the president's cabinet. This showed how important the postal service was.

In 1847 the first two American postage stamps went on sale. One was a five-cent stamp showing Benjamin Franklin's face. The other was a ten-cent stamp with a picture of George Washington on it. People could still choose whether to pay for postage when they sent a letter, or let the receiver pay for it. After 1855, however, people were required to buy stamps to prepay postage.

## Connecting East with West

There were still vast areas of wilderness in America, especially away from the East Coast. Hundreds of miles

The first two American postage stamps, issued in 1847

# ANIMALS AND THE MAIL

Many animals have played a part in the delivery of mail.

In both ancient and modern times, pigeons have been used to send messages. In World War I, a pigeon known as John Silver served the American army in France. Despite being badly injured, the bird managed to carry an important message for some soldiers. He was later honored with a medal.

Another animal on exhibit at the Postal Museum is Owney, the mail dog. Owney wandered into a post office in Albany, New York, in 1888 and decided he liked the mail. At first he rode on the wagons that delivered mail to the railroad station. Later he began riding on the mail trains themselves. Postal workers around the country grew to know and love Owney. He even made some trips with the mail by ship to other countries.

Owney liked to ride with the mail. In Alaska, before airplanes were invented, dog sleds were often the only way to carry mail and other supplies. In some of the most remote northern areas, mail was delivered by reindeer.

You might be surprised to learn that camels have been used to carry mail in the United States. In 1855 Congress bought camels for the army, partly to deliver mail over desert routes in the Southwest. This didn't work out very well, however. A lot of people didn't like the way the camels smelled or the way they spit when they were angry!

There is still a place in the United States today where the mail is delivered by mule train. Deep inside the Grand Canyon is the Havasupai Indian Reservation. The only way in or out of this community is a trail that can be covered by foot, horseback, or mule. Five days a week, a pack of mules takes three to five hours to make the trip down into the canyon. Each mule carries about 200 pounds of mail and other supplies.

As was John Silver, this pigeon used by the U.S. Army is equipped to carry messages.

of mountains, deserts, and thick forests made it difficult for mail to get through to remote settlements. In the early 1800s, if you wanted to send mail from New York to California, it had to go by ship down the Atlantic coast of South America, around Cape Horn, and up the Pacific coast. This could take about six months. To cut this time, ships began to take the mail as far as Panama in Central America, where it was hauled through the jungle by mule, and later by train, to the Pacific coast. There it was loaded on another steamship and sent to California. This reduced mail delivery time from the East Coast to the West Coast to about a month.

It was even more difficult to send mail over land to California. A series of boats, trains, stagecoaches, horse-back riders, and even carriers on foot were used. Mail thieves, hunger, and bad weather were just some of the life-threatening problems that mail carriers faced. More and more people were moving west, however, especially after gold was discovered in California in 1848. They demanded better communication with the folks back east.

A man named William H. Russell came up with a plan. By using the fastest horses and a series of young, light-weight riders, he promised to relay the mail quickly from where the train tracks and telegraph wires ended at St. Joseph, Missouri, to Sacramento, California. The service he developed became known as the Pony Express.

The first ride of the Pony Express began on April 3, 1860. Celebrations were held as the eastbound mail traveled from Sacramento to St. Joseph, and the west-bound mail traveled from St. Joseph to Sacramento in just ten days.

For eighteen months, Pony Express riders carried the mail and helped link the people of the western part of the country with the East. When the stringing of telegraph wires from one end of the country to the other was completed in October 1861, the Pony Express shut down. The telegraph could better take care of short, urgent messages.

## Mail by Rail

There was still a need for mail however, and trains were doing a good job of moving the mail faster. More and more track was being laid. In 1869 the transcontinental railroad was completed. Now mail could be delivered from New York to California in about five to seven days.

Trains were improving mail service in many ways. During the 1860s, railroad postal cars in which mail could be sorted on the move were developed. "Catcher arms" attached to these postal cars could grab a sack of mail hanging outside a railway station as a train passed by without stopping. At the same time, a postal clerk could toss a sack of sorted mail from the train onto the station platform. Soon rail delivery was so efficient that many steamboat and stagecoach routes were eliminated.

## City Mail, Country Mail

In 1863, the postal department began delivering mail to individual homes in large cities free of charge. Another important development that year was the creation of a standard postage rate that didn't depend on the distance mail was traveling.

The use of pneumatic tubes was introduced in 1893 in Philadelphia. In that city's main post office, mail was placed in metal cylinders and dropped into tubes that ran underground. Air pressure pushed the cylinders through the tubes from the main post office to smaller branches. Pneumatic tubes were used in several large cities. They were effectively used in New York City

A worker pulls a bag of mail from the "catcher arm" of the moving train. Moments before, the catcher arm plucked the bag off the mail crane mounted on the ground next to the railroad tracks.

A postal worker fills a metal cylinder with mail. With this method of transporting mail, the cylinder was dropped into a tube that ran underground, and the mail was delivered once it reached its destination.

for over forty years. They were eventually closed down as modern technology found better ways to move the mail.

Improvements were also made in delivering the mail to the many American citizens who did not live in big cities. Most people outside of big cities still had to go to the post office to get their mail. For some farmers, the trip to town and back could take many hours. In bad weather or busy seasons, they might not be able to get their mail for days. Rural free delivery, known as RFD, was introduced in a few places in 1896. It was very popular. Farmers everywhere began asking for RFD in their area. It was difficult for the postal system at first, mostly due to poor roads. As roads were improved,

RFD expanded, and the Postal Service began replacing delivery wagons with automobiles and trucks.

This RFD mail wagon made its rounds about 1908.

## Flying the Mail

One of the first airmail flights was made in September 1911, when a pilot named Earle Ovington flew a sack of mail three miles from Garden City, New York, to Mineola, New York. Ovington flew over a field and dropped the mail to the waiting postmaster.

People were excited about getting mail that had been carried in a plane. In May 1918, the first permanent airmail routes were established between several eastern cities. An airmail rate of twenty-four cents was charged.

At first the planes could fly only during the day. They had no lights, radios, or other instruments to guide them. The pilots often followed railroad tracks, flying low enough to read railroad station signs so they'd know where they were. They often were forced to land in farm fields when weather changed or they ran into other problems.

But now the mail was moving more quickly across the country—by plane during the day and by train at night. This took seventy-two hours (three days), compared to ninety hours (nearly four days) by train alone.

On February 22, 1921, an attempt was made to fly the mail all the way across the country by day and by

The prospect of transporting mail by air was an exciting one, and in 1918 these people gathered to witness the first airmail flight.

On May 13, 1918, stamp collector W. T. Robey went to the post office in Washington, D.C. He wanted to buy some special twenty-four-cent airmail stamps that were being issued. He even took money from his savings account to buy a full sheet of 100 stamps.

As Robey looked at the stamps the clerk gave him, his "heart stood still." He knew what the stamps were supposed to look like, and there was something very wrong with the sheet he held in his hands. On each stamp was a picture of an airplane, but on *these* stamps, the airplanes were all upside down!

As a stamp collector, Robey knew that mistakes could be very valuable. He quietly left the post office. Later he found out that there were no more stamps like his. The Postal Service had been able to destroy all the incorrect stamps except for the sheet that Robey bought.

Four of W. T. Robey's defective airmail stamps, which he originally purchased in 1918

When Robey asked around about the value of his stamps, he was amazed to find that his sheet of stamps was worth thousands of dollars. He finally sold it to a collector in Philadelphia for $15,000.

That sheet of 100 stamps was divided up over the years. Today the location of about eighty of the stamps is known. A group of four of these stamps was purchased in the 1960s for $100,000. They are probably worth even more than that now.

night. Two planes left from San Francisco, heading east, and two left from New York, heading west. One of the eastbound planes crashed near Elko, Nevada, killing the pilot. The others managed to make it to their relay points, where new pilots took over. One pilot, Jack Knight, was supposed to go from North Platte, Nebraska, to Omaha. Since there was no relief pilot waiting when he got there, he refueled and continued on. He flew through blinding snow and fog in the dark of night, but somehow managed to stay on course and landed successfully in Chicago. Another pilot continued the flight from there. The westbound flights were stopped by bad weather. The amazing trip from San Francisco to New York was completed in thirty-three hours and twenty minutes, much faster than the seventy-two hours it took by combining plane and train.

If the mail was going to be carried by plane, and if planes were going to fly at night, improvements were needed. Better landing fields equipped with towers and searchlights were built. Interior and exterior lights were added to planes. These things helped tremendously, but flying the mail was still very dangerous. Between 1918 and 1926, over thirty pilots were killed in plane accidents.

Pilots sometimes joked about the danger. After a crash landing, a pilot named Dean Smith sent this telegram: FLYING LOW. ENGINE QUIT. ONLY PLACE TO LAND ON COW. KILLED COW. WRECKED PLANE. SCARED ME.

In the mid-1920s, airline companies were given contracts to fly the mail for the government. These airlines were able to benefit from the safety features that had been developed by the Postal Service. This was a big boost to the development of many of the airlines that are in business today. By 1931, air transportation had cut the time for a letter to travel from coast to coast down to about twenty-eight hours. Today it takes less than five hours.

# THE POSTAL SERVICE TODAY

Most of early postal history involves changes in how mail was moved from one part of the country to another. In more recent decades, many of the changes have involved the ways in which the mail is sorted and processed.

## The Information Age

We live in a time that is known as the Information Age. One of the greatest tools of the Information Age is the computer. Since about the 1960s, computers have affected almost every aspect of life in America. They have had a tremendous impact on the Postal Service.

For one thing, computers greatly increased the amount of mail that businesses could produce. More postal workers were hired, but in many places, especially large cities, it became difficult to move the mail quickly. A number of plans were proposed to handle all that mail. One was the Zoning Improvement Plan, developed in 1963. Five-number codes known as ZIP Codes were introduced to help postal employees sort mail faster.

The dawning of the Information Age in the 1960s meant that the postal system needed to undergo great changes. The postal system we know today was born in 1971.

But ZIP Codes were not enough. Major changes were needed to solve the problems the postal system faced. A reorganization plan was signed by President Richard Nixon on August 12, 1970.

## The New Postal Service

On July 1, 1971, the new Postal Service was born. It completely changed the way the postal system operated. The postmaster general would no longer be part of the president's cabinet. Instead, he would work with nine governors who would run the Postal Service more like a business. Now the Postal Service is an independent agency within the executive branch of the U.S. government.

At the same time, the Postal Service was experimenting with machines to make mail sorting quicker. Today postal workers use a variety of computers and other types of electronic machinery to speed the mail-sorting process.

In 1983 the ZIP Code was updated to the ZIP + 4, the usual five-digit code plus four additional digits, mostly for areas with many businesses. The dependable and efficient delivery of business mail has always been a high priority with the Postal Service. Many of the improvements in speed of delivery over the years were made with businesses in mind.

## How Does Mail Processing Work?

Suppose you want to mail a letter to a friend who lives in another city. Maybe you live where you can put it in your own personal mailbox outside your front door or at the end of your driveway. You put up a flag on your

Whether mail is picked up from a private mailbox or a U.S. Postal Service collection box, it all travels to the local post office and then to a postal plant for processing.

mailbox to tell the mail carrier you are sending mail and he or she picks up your letter when your mail is dropped off. Or you might leave your letter in a mail collection box at a shopping center or on a busy corner where a postal worker comes by several times a day. Or maybe you take it straight to the post office and drop it in the "out of town" mail slot. Once the letter is at your local post office, it goes into a sack that gets sent to a postal plant for processing. Trucks arrive at the plants day and night, carrying sacks of mail from local post offices all over the area.

Today postal plants use high-speed equipment to process the mail. Sacks of mail are emptied onto conveyor belts. The largest packages and envelopes are removed to be handled separately. The rest go on to the facer-canceller, which faces the envelopes all in the same direction, so that the stamps are on top in the upper right-hand corner. The stamps are then canceled. This means they have dark lines printed across them so they can't be used again. Then a postmark is printed on the envelope. Postmarks are usually round, with the location of the plant and the date printed on them.

Then the letter is ready to begin the sorting process. It may go to an optical character reader (OCR). The OCR has an electric eye that reads the address and then sprays a bar code on the envelope. Bar codes are tiny straight black lines that represent information—in this case, an address. The OCR can read and spray bar codes on about 500 letters a minute. But it can only read certain kinds of printing, like that done by computers.

Bar code sorters sort the letters that the OCR could read by region. Other letters go on to other types of letter-sorting machines. Postal workers read the ZIP code on the letter and type it into the machine. Then the letter is moved into a bin with other letters going to the same region.

Letters that are staying in this postal plant's region get further sorted by destination post office and get sent to the appropriate post office by truck. Mail going to another region usually gets taken by truck to the nearest airport to be sent to the appropriate region. It is then sorted and delivered to local post offices.

Once the mail gets to the recipient's local post office, individual mail carriers sort the mail for their routes. They use a case with slots called "pigeon holes." The mail ends up organized in the order in which it will be delivered.

Finally the mail is delivered. In small towns or rural areas, mail carriers may use a car or some other special vehicle to deliver the mail. In most cities, the mail carrier delivers the mail mainly on foot, although he or she may have a special cart to help carry the mail.

This interior shot of an optical character reader (OCR) shows the lens and the illumination system used to read the address on a piece of mail.

A mail carrier is responsible for arranging the mail for his or her route in the order in which it will be delivered.

People without a permanent address can ask a particular post office to collect and hold their mail for them to pick up. This is called "general delivery."

When mail can't be delivered for some reason, the post office will look at the return address to try to return it to the person who sent it. If this isn't possible, it goes to the dead letter office. There the mail might be opened for clues to find out who it belongs to.

## The Local Post Office

The local post office is a busy place. In the customer service area, there is a counter where people can have packages weighed and buy stamps, postcards, money orders, and other postal goods. Some post offices handle other government services, too, such as issuing food stamps and taking passport applications.

Clerks who work at these counters have to keep careful track of everything they sell. All the money they collect is used to help operate the U.S. Postal Service.

Most post offices have a lobby area with mailboxes that can be rented. Some people get their mail delivered to these "P. O. Boxes." They will have a key or combination to open their locked mailboxes. Usually this lobby area is open longer than the customer service area.

Then there is the "back" area of the post office. This is where local mail is sorted and prepared for delivery. Mail dropped off at this post office is prepared to head on to a plant. Mail traffic is always busy, coming and going.

## Competition

The Postal Service faces competition from new technologies like e-mail and fax machines that can deliver messages very quickly. It also competes with private companies like United Parcel Service (UPS) and Federal Express (FedEx). These companies cannot deliver regular mail. But like the Postal Service, they can charge fees to deliver urgent mail and packages. When UPS workers went on strike during the summer of 1997, many post offices found themselves handling a greatly increased load of packages.

The Postal Service is always trying to improve service. Like all businesses, the Postal Service has to work hard at improving service while holding down costs.

Today the seal of the Postal Service is an eagle over the words "U.S. Mail," surrounded by the words "United States Postal Service" and nine stars. This symbol was created when the post office was reorganized in 1970. It replaced a seal that showed a post rider on horseback.

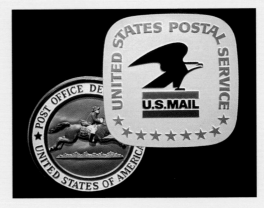

The current seal of the United States Postal Service (right), in use since 1971, replaced a seal that had been introduced in the 1860s (left).

Americans want mail delivered in a reasonable amount of time and at a reasonable cost. According to surveys, many Americans believe that mail service is a bargain when compared to a variety of other services, such as telephone service, electricity, public transportation, and hospital care.

Today we have a choice of many ways to communicate. For millions of messages each day, the Postal Service is still the way to go.

# PEOPLE BEHIND
# THE MAIL

The United States Postal Service (USPS) is one of the world's largest businesses. Making it work is a huge job. Some 750,000 employees play a part in getting the mail through. This makes the USPS the nation's largest employer after the military.

## The Board of Governors

Since its reorganization in 1971, the USPS has been run by a board of nine governors. Each serves for nine years. Each year, one member's term expires and the president of the United States appoints a new member. If the Senate agrees to the president's choice, that member then joins the board of governors for nine years.

The governors select a postmaster general, and then a deputy postmaster general is selected. Together, these eleven individuals run the Postal Service as the board of governors.

## Postmasters

The postmaster general provides leadership for the Postal Service. The postmaster general has to understand the business of this huge government agency. The postmaster general also has to deal well with the many other people who work for the Postal Service.

Some of the people who report to the postmaster general are regional vice presidents. Below them are district managers and postmasters of local post offices. All these positions require dedicated, hard-working individuals to do the work and make the decisions necessary to get the mail through.

## Other Employees

Some of the jobs in the Postal Service include: city and rural mail carriers, customer service clerks, mail sorters, and machinery maintenance workers. A variety of skills are needed to work for the Postal Service. Some employees need to be strong enough to deal with heavy

Mail carriers must be prepared to do their job in all kinds of weather.

sacks of mail. Mail carriers and some others have to tolerate bad weather of all sorts. Many postal workers have to be able to work at night. Customer service clerks need skills in dealing with people and handling questions and complaints. Many postal workers today need to be able to use computers and other expensive high-tech machinery.

## Famous Postal Workers

A few postal workers have become famous for the way they did their jobs. One of these was a man named John Thompson. In 1856 he began carrying the mail to miners in the Sierra Nevada Mountains. These miners had been unable to receive mail all winter long because no one could get through the deep drifts of snow. But Thompson, who was born in Norway, knew how to travel *over* the snow. He made himself a pair of skis from an oak tree and soon he was known as Snowshoe Thompson. On the coldest days and darkest nights, he carried the mail through the mountain passes, keeping the miners in touch with the rest of the world.

This, the earliest known photograph of Abraham Lincoln, was made in 1846, about ten years after he served as postmaster of New Salem, Illinois.

Some postal workers have gone on to become famous at other things. At least two went on to become president of the United States. Abraham Lincoln was postmaster of New Salem, Illinois, when he was twenty-four years old. He served in that job for three years. He is said to have personally delivered mail to customers by carrying it in his hat. Harry

Harry S. Truman

U.S. Postage 8 cents

After his death in 1972, former president and postmaster of Grandview, Missouri, Harry S. Truman was honored with a postage stamp issued by the U.S. Postal Service.

S. Truman, who would become president in 1945, was appointed postmaster of Grandview, Missouri, when he was a young man.

William Faulkner, who would become a famous writer, did not do so well as postmaster of the University of Mississippi Post Office. He was accused of refusing to sort mail, being rude to customers, and playing cards on the job.

## Postal Inspection Service

Did you know that only postal workers (or the person to whom mail is addressed) may remove mail from a mailbox? This and other postal laws are enforced by the Postal Inspection Service. The Postal Inspection Service is a federal law enforcement agency. Like many other law enforcement agencies, its inspectors wear badges and carry guns. Their job is to make things safe for postal employees and to protect post office property and the mail. They are on the lookout for mail fraud, stolen mail, and bombs, guns, drugs, or other illegal materials in the mail. There are sometimes rewards offered to people who help postal inspectors solve crimes.

If postal inspectors want to open suspicious mail, they have to ask a judge for a search warrant. Only employees of the dead letter office, or people who have a search warrant, may open a letter that is not ad-

# A FEW POSTMASTERS TO KNOW

Samuel Osgood was the first postmaster general after the United States Constitution became law. He was appointed by President George Washington in 1789. He worked hard to get the U.S. postal system off to a good start. When he became postmaster general, there were seventy-five post offices, connected by 2,000 miles of post roads. Many of these post offices were just a corner of a shop or inn. Many of the roads were more like paths or trails through forests or swamps.

Postmaster General Montgomery Blair was appointed by President Abraham Lincoln in 1861. He had the difficult job of overseeing the postal system during the Civil War. One of his important contributions was the creation of postal money orders in 1864. These worked like checks and made it easier for soldiers to send money home to their families. Blair also worked hard to improve the delivery of mail between the United States and other countries.

Marvin Runyon became postmaster general in 1992. He had been a successful business manager before taking this important job with the Postal Service. In 1993 he helped the Postal Service cut costs so that postage rates did not have to go up. In 1998 he announced that he would be leaving his job with the Postal Service. The governors would have to choose someone new.

dressed to them. Postal inspectors can x-ray the inside of a letter or package they think might be dangerous. It is against the law to mail anything that might seriously hurt someone.

Next time you drop a letter in the mail, maybe you'll take a minute to think about all the men and women, machines and vehicles that it will take to get it to its destination.

# CHAPTER

★ 5

# IN THE MAIL

Now that you know all about what happens to a letter once it's mailed, and how the Postal Service came to be, are you more interested than before in using this service? If so, that's great. Writing letters is a good habit to get into. Putting your thoughts and feelings down on paper can help you organize your thinking, as well as improve your communication skills.

## Letters Make a Difference

In 1860 a young girl named Grace Bedell wrote a letter to the new president, Abraham Lincoln. Among other things, she mentioned that she thought he should grow a beard. Up to that time, Abraham Lincoln had never worn a beard. Not only did Mr. Lincoln write back to Grace, he decided to try growing a beard. He wore one the rest of his life.

Another girl, Samantha Smith, wrote a letter to the head of the former Soviet Union, Yuri Andropov, in 1982. She asked Mr. Andropov why the Soviets wanted war with the United States. A few months later, Sam-

In 1982, ten-year-old Samantha Smith used her letter-writing skills to communicate with the head of the Soviet Union, Yuri Andropov.

During the Persian Gulf War (1991), many Americans wanted to show their support for the servicemen and women who joined the effort to free Kuwait from Iraqi control. One way they could do this was by sending a huge number of letters and packages to the armed forces.

Many people in the military would agree that one of the keys to keeping spirits high among the troops is the exchange of mail with those they've left behind. During Desert Storm, as the Persian Gulf War was called, many people, especially schoolchildren, who didn't personally know anyone in the service, sent letters addressed to "any serviceman." These letters were distributed among the troops and gratefully received.

Many of the letter writers received personal responses from soldiers they didn't know before. Some of the servicemen and women also wrote to the Postal Service, thanking them for their part in creating this connection between the American people and the armed forces.

A soldier in the Persian Gulf War reads a letter on board his ship. Many people, even those who did not know someone in the service, wrote letters addressed to "any serviceman."

antha received a reply from the Russian leader, explaining that his people wanted peace, and inviting her to come there to see for herself. Samantha visited Russia,

and then shared the message of peace with many people. Letters can make a difference!

## Stamps

In 1847 the United States Post Office began selling postage stamps. Some people had a hard time learning how to use these stamps. Sometimes they licked the glue right off the stamp and then they got mad when the stamps would not stick to their letters!

Today there are mainly two kinds of stamps issued in the United States. They are called "regular" issues and "commemoratives." Regular stamps are printed in large quantities and are reprinted when supplies run

A philatelist (stamp collector) will buy an entire sheet of stamps like this one that depicts musical legends such as Elvis Presley and Buddy Holly.

low. They are the stamps you see most often on every-day business and personal mail.

Commemoratives are specially designed to honor a person or remember an event. They are usually not reprinted when the supply runs out. Though they can be used for everyday mail, they are the stamps that collectors often buy to keep. The United States issued its first commemorative stamps in 1893, to honor the World's Fair that was held in Chicago that year. Today the Postal Service issues about a dozen new commemorative stamps each year.

Altogether, billions of regular and commemorative stamps are sold by the United States Postal Service each year. They are printed at the Bureau of Engraving and Printing in Washington, D.C. This is also where our country's paper money is printed.

A group called the Citizen's Stamp Advisory Committee recommends subjects for stamps to the postmaster general. Citizens can make suggestions to the committee. President Franklin Roosevelt, who enjoyed stamps, made a number of his own suggestions, some of which actually became stamps.

There are many rules for the designs and pictures on stamps. American law states that no living person can be pictured on a U.S. postal stamp. Even American presidents don't get their pictures on stamps until after they die.

## Stamp Collecting

As the use of stamps caught on, some people began to buy stamps for collections. In time, stamp collecting became one of the most popular hobbies in the world.

The fancy name for stamp collecting is philately. People who collect and study stamps are philatelists.

Most stamp collectors keep their stamps in a special album, so they can look at their stamps without damaging them. They might collect stamps that come on the mail delivered to their house. They can also buy stamps at the post office or through catalogs.

There are many, many kinds of stamps. Some people collect stamps from different countries. Others collect stamps with pictures of something they are interested in, like sports or flowers. Others might collect stamps that show pictures of famous people or important events. There are many books you can read if you are interested in learning more about stamp collecting.

## An Important Service

Collecting stamps can be an interesting way to learn about the world. Learning about the Postal Service is an interesting way to learn about our country. From cutting paths through the wilderness to paving airplane runways, the United States Postal Service has helped America grow. It has also helped Americans communicate with each other. And while Benjamin Franklin and Samuel Osgood would probably be amazed at all the changes in the Postal Service and in America since their day, they would not be surprised to see how important the Postal Service is to us.

# Chronology

| | |
|---|---|
| **1639** | The tavern of Richard Fairbanks in Boston becomes the first official post office in the colonies. |
| **1775** | The Continental Congress appoints Benjamin Franklin as postmaster general. |
| **1789** | George Washington names Samuel Osgood as the first postmaster general under the U.S. Constitution. |
| **1829** | President Andrew Jackson makes the postmaster general part of his cabinet. |
| **1847** | The first U.S. postage stamps are issued. |
| **1855** | Prepayment with postage stamps becomes mandatory. |
| **1860–1861** | The Pony Express delivers mail between St. Joseph, Missouri, and Sacramento, California. |
| **1863** | The post office begins free delivery of mail to individual homes in cities. Postage charges are based on weight of mail rather than distance carried. |
| **1864** | Special railroad cars are developed to sort mail on the move. |
| **1896** | Rural free delivery (RFD) is begun. |
| **1911** | Earle Ovington experiments with flying the mail. |

**1918**    First regular airmail flights are scheduled during the
            day between several cities in the East.

**1921**    Mail is flown across the country, traveling day and
            night.

**1963**    ZIP Codes are created to help make mail sorting
            easier and faster.

**1970**    The Postal Reorganization Act is signed.

**1971**    The Postal Department becomes the United States
            Postal Service, an independent establishment of
            the executive branch of the federal government.
            The postmaster general is no longer a member of
            the cabinet.

**1980s**   Electronic sorting machines, including optical
            character readers (OCRs) help speed mail
            processing.

**1983**    ZIP+4 helps further speed business mail
            processing.

# For Further Reading

Bolick, Nancy O'Keefe. *Mail Call! The History of the U.S. Postal Service*. New York: Franklin Watts, 1994.

Briggs, Michael. *Hobby Handbooks: Stamps*. New York: Random House, 1992.

Dicerto, Joseph J. *The Pony Express, Hoofbeats in the Wilderness*. New York: Franklin Watts, 1989.

James, Elizabeth, and Carol Barkin. *Sincerely Yours, How to Write Great Letters*. New York: Clarion Books, 1993.

McAfee, Cheryl Weant. *Know Your Government: The United States Postal Service*. New York: Chelsea House, 1987.

Mischel, Florence D. *How to Write a Letter*. New York: Franklin Watts, 1988.

United States Postal Service. *History of the United States Postal Service*. Washington, D.C., 1993.

## Places to Write and Visit

National Postal Museum
Smithsonian Institution
2 Massachusetts Avenue, NE
Washington D.C. 20560-0001

Museum of Postal History
General Post Office
421 Eighth Avenue
New York NY 10199

Junior Philatelists of America
P.O. Box 850
Boalsburg PA 16827-0850
Website: www.jpastamps.org

Postal Service Web Site
www.usps.gov

# Index